Retiree: _____

Retirement Date: _____

Memories and Stories...

Guest: _____

Memories and Stories:

_____
_____
_____
_____
_____

Guest: _____

Memories and Stories:

_____
_____
_____
_____
_____

Guest: _____

Memories and Stories:

_____
_____
_____
_____
_____

Guest: _____

Memories and Stories:

_____
_____
_____
_____
_____

Guest: _____

Memories and Stories:

_____
_____
_____
_____
_____

Guest: _____

Memories and Stories:

_____
_____
_____
_____
_____

Words of Appreciation

Guest: _____

Words of Appreciation:
_____
_____
_____
_____
_____

Guest: _____

Words of Appreciation:
_____
_____
_____
_____
_____

Guest: _____

Words of Appreciation:
_____
_____
_____
_____
_____

Guest: _____

Words of Appreciation:
_____
_____
_____
_____
_____

Guest: _____

Words of Appreciation:
_____
_____
_____
_____
_____

Guest: _____

Words of Appreciation:
_____
_____
_____
_____
_____

Well Wishes and Advice

Guest: _____

Well Wishes and Advice:
_____
_____
_____
_____
_____

Guest: _____

Well Wishes and Advice:
_____
_____
_____
_____
_____

Guest: _____

Well Wishes and Advice:
_____
_____
_____
_____
_____

Guest: _____

Well Wishes and Advice:
_____
_____
_____
_____
_____

Guest: _____

Well Wishes and Advice:
_____
_____
_____
_____
_____

Guest: _____

Well Wishes and Advice:
_____
_____
_____
_____
_____

Funny Memories

Guest: _____

Funny Memories:
_____
_____
_____
_____
_____

Guest: _____

Funny Memories:
_____
_____
_____
_____
_____

Guest: _____

Funny Memories:
_____
_____
_____
_____
_____

Guest: _____

Funny Memories:
_____
_____
_____
_____
_____

Guest: _____

Funny Memories:
_____
_____
_____
_____
_____

Guest: _____

Funny Memories:
_____
_____
_____
_____
_____

Memories and Stories...

Guest:

Memories and Stories:

Guest:

Memories and Stories:

Guest:

Memories and Stories:

Guest:

Memories and Stories:

Guest:

Memories and Stories:

Guest:

Memories and Stories:

Memories and Stories...

Guest: _____

Memories and Stories:
_____
_____
_____
_____

Guest: _____

Memories and Stories:
_____
_____
_____
_____

Guest: _____

Memories and Stories:
_____
_____
_____
_____

Guest: _____

Memories and Stories:
_____
_____
_____
_____

Guest: _____

Memories and Stories:
_____
_____
_____
_____

Guest: _____

Memories and Stories:
_____
_____
_____
_____

Words of Appreciation

Guest: _____

Words of Appreciation:

_____
_____
_____
_____
_____

Guest: _____

Words of Appreciation:

_____
_____
_____
_____
_____

Guest: _____

Words of Appreciation:

_____
_____
_____
_____
_____

Guest: _____

Words of Appreciation:

_____
_____
_____
_____
_____

Words of Appreciation:

_____
_____
_____
_____
_____

Guest: _____

Words of Appreciation:

_____
_____
_____
_____
_____

Words of Appreciation

Guest: _____

Words of Appreciation:
_____
_____
_____
_____
_____

Guest: _____

Words of Appreciation:
_____
_____
_____
_____
_____

Guest: _____

Words of Appreciation:
_____
_____
_____
_____
_____

Guest: _____

Words of Appreciation:
_____
_____
_____
_____
_____

Guest: _____

Words of Appreciation:
_____
_____
_____
_____
_____

Guest: _____

Words of Appreciation:
_____
_____
_____
_____
_____

Well Wishes and Advice

Guest: _____

Well Wishes and Advice:

_____
_____
_____
_____
_____

Guest: _____

Well Wishes and Advice:

_____
_____
_____
_____
_____

Guest: _____

Well Wishes and Advice:

_____
_____
_____
_____
_____

Guest: _____

Well Wishes and Advice:

_____
_____
_____
_____
_____

Guest: _____

Well Wishes and Advice:

_____
_____
_____
_____
_____

Guest: _____

Well Wishes and Advice:

_____
_____
_____
_____
_____

Funny Memories

Guest: _____

Funny Memories:
_____
_____
_____
_____
_____

Guest: _____

Funny Memories:
_____
_____
_____
_____
_____

Guest: _____

Funny Memories:
_____
_____
_____
_____
_____

Guest: _____

Funny Memories:
_____
_____
_____
_____
_____

Guest: _____

Funny Memories:
_____
_____
_____
_____
_____

Guest: _____

Funny Memories:
_____
_____
_____
_____
_____

Memories and Stories...

Guest:

Memories and Stories:

Guest:

Memories and Stories:

Guest:

Memories and Stories:

Guest:

Memories and Stories:

Guest:

Memories and Stories:

Guest:

Memories and Stories:

Funny Memories

Guest: _____

Funny Memories:

_____
_____
_____
_____

Guest: _____

Funny Memories:

_____
_____
_____
_____

Guest: _____

Funny Memories:

_____
_____
_____
_____

Guest: _____

Funny Memories:

_____
_____
_____
_____

Guest: _____

Funny Memories:

_____
_____
_____
_____

Guest: _____

Funny Memories:

_____
_____
_____
_____

Well Wishes and Advice

Guest:

Well Wishes and Advice:

Guest:

Well Wishes and Advice:

Guest:

Well Wishes and Advice:

Guest:

Well Wishes and Advice:

Guest:

Well Wishes and Advice:

Guest:

Well Wishes and Advice:

Funny Memories

Guest: _____

Funny Memories:

_____
_____
_____
_____
_____

Guest: _____

Funny Memories:

_____
_____
_____
_____
_____

Guest: _____

Funny Memories:

_____
_____
_____
_____
_____

Guest: _____

Funny Memories:

_____
_____
_____
_____
_____

Guest: _____

Funny Memories:

_____
_____
_____
_____
_____

Guest: _____

Funny Memories:

_____
_____
_____
_____
_____

Well Wishes and Advice

Guest:

Well Wishes and Advice:

_____
_____
_____
_____

Guest:

Well Wishes and Advice:

_____
_____
_____
_____

Guest:

Well Wishes and Advice:

_____
_____
_____
_____

Guest:

Well Wishes and Advice:

_____
_____
_____
_____

Guest:

Well Wishes and Advice:

_____
_____
_____
_____

Guest:

Well Wishes and Advice:

_____
_____
_____
_____

Memories and Stories...

Guest:

Memories and Stories:

Guest:

Memories and Stories:

Guest:

Memories and Stories:

Guest:

Memories and Stories:

Guest:

Memories and Stories:

Guest:

Memories and Stories:

Words of Appreciation

Guest:

Words of Appreciation:

Guest:

Words of Appreciation:

Guest:

Words of Appreciation:

Guest:

Words of Appreciation:

Guest:

Words of Appreciation:

Guest:

Words of Appreciation:

Words of Appreciation

Guest:

Words of Appreciation:

Guest:

Words of Appreciation:

Guest:

Words of Appreciation:

Guest:

Words of Appreciation:

Guest:

Words of Appreciation:

Guest:

Words of Appreciation:

Well Wishes and Advice

Guest:

Well Wishes and Advice:

Guest:

Well Wishes and Advice:

Guest:

Well Wishes and Advice:

Guest:

Well Wishes and Advice:

Guest:

Well Wishes and Advice:

Guest:

Well Wishes and Advice:

Words of Appreciation

Guest: _____

Words of Appreciation:
_____
_____
_____
_____
_____

Guest: _____

Words of Appreciation:
_____
_____
_____
_____
_____

Guest: _____

Words of Appreciation:
_____
_____
_____
_____
_____

Guest: _____

Words of Appreciation:
_____
_____
_____
_____
_____

Guest: _____

Words of Appreciation:
_____
_____
_____
_____
_____

Guest: _____

Words of Appreciation:
_____
_____
_____
_____
_____

Memories and Stories...

Guest:

Memories and Stories:

Guest:

Memories and Stories:

Guest:

Memories and Stories:

Guest:

Memories and Stories:

Guest:

Memories and Stories:

Guest:

Memories and Stories:

Well Wishes and Advice

Guest: _____

Well Wishes and Advice:
_____
_____
_____
_____

Guest: _____

Well Wishes and Advice:
_____
_____
_____
_____

Guest: _____

Well Wishes and Advice:
_____
_____
_____
_____

Guest: _____

Well Wishes and Advice:
_____
_____
_____
_____

Guest: _____

Well Wishes and Advice:
_____
_____
_____
_____

Guest: _____

Well Wishes and Advice:
_____
_____
_____
_____

Funny Memories

Guest: _____

Funny Memories:
_____
_____
_____
_____
_____

Guest: _____

Funny Memories:
_____
_____
_____
_____
_____

Guest: _____

Funny Memories:
_____
_____
_____
_____
_____

Guest: _____

Funny Memories:
_____
_____
_____
_____
_____

Guest: _____

Funny Memories:
_____
_____
_____
_____
_____

Guest: _____

Funny Memories:
_____
_____
_____
_____
_____

Funny Memories

Guest: _____

Funny Memories:
_____
_____
_____
_____
_____

Guest: _____

Funny Memories:
_____
_____
_____
_____
_____

Guest: _____

Funny Memories:
_____
_____
_____
_____
_____

Guest: _____

Funny Memories:
_____
_____
_____
_____
_____

Guest: _____

Funny Memories:
_____
_____
_____
_____
_____

Guest: _____

Funny Memories:
_____
_____
_____
_____
_____

Thank you for your thoughts and well wishes! Looking forward to exciting adventures ahead... 🤎🤎💛🤍

www.ingramcontent.com/pod-product-compliance
Lightning Source LLC
Chambersburg PA
CBHW051515110526
44582CB00007B/134